WITHDRAWN

What's the Buzz?

KEEPING BEES IN FLIGHT

MERRIE-ELLEN WILCOX

ORCA BOOK PUBLISHERS

Library and Archives Canada Cataloguing in Publication

Wilcox, Merrie-Ellen, author
What's the buzz? : keeping bees in flight / Merrie-Ellen Wilcox.
(Orca footprints)

Includes index.
Issued in print and electronic formats.
ISBN 978-1-4598-0960-4 (bound).—ISBN 978-1-4598-0961-1 (pdf).—
ISBN 978-1-4598-0962-8 (epub)

1. Bees—Juvenile literature. I. Title. II. Series: Orca footprints

QL565.2.W54 2015   j595.79'9   c2015-901562-6
                    c2015-901563-4

First published in the United States, 2015
Library of Congress Control Number: 2015934244

Summary: Part of the nonfiction Footprints series for middle readers, illustrated with many color photographs. Readers will discover why bees are important and how people are working to save them.

Orca Book Publishers is dedicated to preserving the environment and has printed this book on Forest Stewardship Council® certified paper.

Orca Book Publishers gratefully acknowledges the support for its publishing programs provided by the following agencies: the Government of Canada through the Canada Book Fund and the Canada Council for the Arts, and the Province of British Columbia through the BC Arts Council and the Book Publishing Tax Credit.

Front cover images by Adrianam13/dreamstime.com and Mordolff/istock.com
Back cover images: top left to right: Blickwinkel/Alamy, Kriz Partridge/Bee Against Monsanto, Christopher Butterfield; bottom left to right: Deb Alperin/gettyimages.com, Atarel/dreamstime.com, hsvrs/istock.com

Design and production by Teresa Bubela and Jenn Playford

ORCA BOOK PUBLISHERS
www.orcabook.com

Printed and bound in Canada.

18 17 16 15 • 4 3 2 1

A honey bee returning to her hive, laden with pollen.
ADRIANAM13/DREAMSTIME.COM

For Christopher, who brought bees into our life, and for Akai,
whose curiosity about them was the reason for this book.

Contents

CHAPTER ONE:
A WORLD OF BEES

CHAPTER TWO:
BEES AT WORK

CHAPTER THREE:
LIFE IN THE HIVE

CHAPTER FOUR:
KEEPING THE BEES IN FLIGHT

Introduction

Early one summer morning a few years ago, I loaded my first beehive into the back of my car near where I live in Victoria, British Columbia. John, the beekeeper who sold it to me, had plugged the entrance, but a few bees that had already left the hive were now coming back with pollen and nectar and trying to get into their home. I got the giggles as I drove home with a car full of honey bees—several thousand of them safely inside the hive, but quite a few that were flying around in the car!

This is me beside one of the beehives in my garden. CHRISTOPHER BUTTERFIELD

John and I carried the hive to a sunny spot in the garden and opened up the entrance. He gave me an old beekeeper's veil to protect my head, leather gloves for my hands, and a hive tool to use for moving things around in the hive. Then he took off the lid and gave me my first lesson in beekeeping. After that, I was on my own.

Many mistakes and only a few stings later, I now have six hives. And I have learned so much—not just about honey bees, but also about all the wild bees that live with us and how much we depend on them. I've also learned how human activities have harmed them, and how badly they now need our help to survive.

This book will take you into the busy world of bees. You don't need a veil or gloves to be amazed—just come with me!

Connor and Andrew are learning about beekeeping at their school in Portland, Oregon. NADINE FIEDLER/CATLIN GABEL SCHOOL

All Abuzz

When I was growing up in Ontario, we always had clover honey in early summer. It was pale and clear, with a mild flavor, and sometimes we got it right in the wax honeycomb, to chew like candy. In the fall, we had buckwheat honey, almost black and very strong tasting, and especially good on pumpkin pie at Thanksgiving! Later, when I started traveling, I noticed that honey from different places looked and tasted different. That's because the color and taste of the honey depend on the flowers that the bees have visited, and every place has different kinds of plants.

These jars of honey taste as different as they look. FOREWER/SHUTTERSTOCK.COM

CHAPTER ONE

A World of Bees

BEES, BEES AND MORE BEES

Lots of people think that anything that buzzes and has black and yellow stripes is a bee, and that all bees sting. Many stinging insects with stripes aren't bees at all—they are wasps. And many bees don't have stripes and don't sting!

There are about 20,000 known species of bees in the world. That's more than all of the species of birds and mammals combined.

Bees live on every continent except Antarctica. Every place has particular kinds of bees that live there. These are called "native" bees. Some species live in a very large area, or range, while others are found only in one small area, like an island.

About 4,000 species of bees are native to North America. On Vancouver Island, where I live, there are about 100 species of native bees. You might be amazed at how many bee species live in your area.

Bees are incredibly diverse. Some are so small—about two millimeters long—that you can't really see them without a magnifying glass. And the world's biggest bee, called Wallace's giant bee, is 39 millimeters (1.5 inches) long and has a wingspan of almost twice that, at 63 millimeters (2.5 inches)!

A girl examines a bee through a magnifying glass. BLICKWINKEL/ALAMY

Bees come in many shapes and sizes. The leafcutter bee in the center has cut and rolled up a leaf to use in her nest.
ROB CRUICKSHANK; ROB CRUICKSHANK; CHRISTOPHER BUTTERFIELD

Bees range in color from black to red to metallic green or blue. Some have stripes, and some seem to change color as they move and catch the light, like a jewel.

BEES ARE NOT WASPS!

Bees evolved from wasps about 100 million years ago, around the time that flowering plants were becoming the most common type of vegetation on Earth. Wasps are hunters and *carnivores*: they kill other insects, including bees, and feed them to their young. (Have you noticed that they will also eat some of your hamburger or fish at a barbecue or picnic?) Bees are vegetarians: they rely on pollen and *nectar* from flowering plants to feed themselves and their young.

Because of this basic difference in what they do, bees and wasps have some different body parts. For example, bees have hairs that help them gather and carry pollen, so they often look quite furry. Wasps are usually smoother. Many female bees also have a special structure for carrying pollen—either a patch of long, stiff hairs (called a *scopa*) or a pollen basket (a *corbicula*) on their back legs. And bees have long tongues for gathering nectar from flowers.

BEE FACT: A few bumble bee species live in the Arctic regions of North America, Europe and Asia, where not many other bees can live. In the Arctic summer it is light twenty-four hours a day, so the bees work around the clock to make up for the short summer and very long winter.

A wasp kills a honey bee. It will carry the bee back to its nest to feed to its young.
KUTSUKS/ISTOCK.COM

9

A honey bee grows from a tiny egg to larva to pupa to full-grown bee in 21 days. ERIC TOURNERET

Another important physical difference between bees and wasps is their waists. Bees have a thicker waist than wasps, whose waist can be as thin as a needle. This is an easy way to tell them apart. It's good to know the difference between bees and wasps, especially for people who might be allergic to one or the other.

A BUG'S LIFE

Like all insects, a bee has a head, a *thorax* and an *abdomen*. On its head are five eyes—two big *compound eyes*, each consisting of many separate lenses, and three simple eyes, called *ocelli*—and two very sensitive *antennae*, as well as that long tongue for gathering nectar and strong jaws for chewing. Its six legs and two pairs of wings are attached to its thorax, the middle section. The abdomen is where things like the special glands for making wax are, and, in stinging bees, the stinger.

Bees also have the same life cycle as other insects, called *metamorphosis*. They start as an egg. A *larva* hatches from the egg. It looks like a grub and feeds on food in the nest. The larva then spins a *cocoon* around itself and becomes a *pupa*. Inside the cocoon, the pupa gradually develops all the body parts of a bee. What emerges from the cocoon is an adult bee.

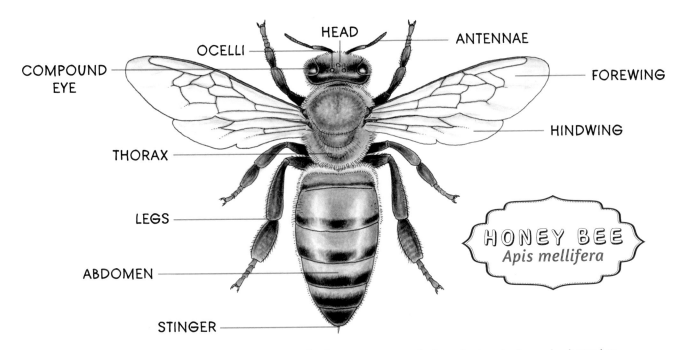

OCELLI

HEAD

ANTENNAE

COMPOUND EYE

FOREWING

HINDWING

THORAX

LEGS

HONEY BEE
Apis mellifera

ABDOMEN

STINGER

Bees usually don't stay still long enough to be examined. Here you can see the important parts of a worker honey bee.
NOEL BADGES PUGH FROM *FIELD GUIDE TO THE BEES OF CALIFORNIA*, BY GRETCHEN LEBUHN (UNIVERSITY OF CALIFORNIA PRESS)

SOCIAL OR SOLITARY?

Some bees live in groups or colonies. A colony might consist of as few as two adult females or, in the case of honey bees, as many as 60,000 bees living together and sharing the work of preparing the nest and providing food for the young. *Entomologists* (people who study insects) call these bees "social bees."

But by far the majority of bees—about 90 percent of the native bees in North America—are solitary bees. Each female bee makes a nest and provides a store of food for her eggs without any help from others. Some solitary bees build their nests in groups, but each nest still contains only one female and her offspring, which might number just a few for some species to a few dozen for others.

HOME SWEET HOME

Both solitary and social bees also live in different kinds of homes.

For example, mining bees make their nests in holes that they dig in the ground. Some dig in sandy soils, others in clay;

A solitary native bee peers out of her home.
ROB CRUICKSHANK

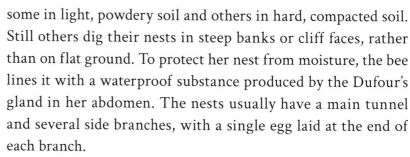

some in light, powdery soil and others in hard, compacted soil. Still others dig their nests in steep banks or cliff faces, rather than on flat ground. To protect her nest from moisture, the bee lines it with a waterproof substance produced by the Dufour's gland in her abdomen. The nests usually have a main tunnel and several side branches, with a single egg laid at the end of each branch.

Other bees make their homes in spaces or tunnels that either were made by others, like beetles, or occur naturally, like plant stems and hollow trees. Leafcutter bees line their nests with pieces of leaves that they cut and then glue together to form a cylinder or sphere. Mason bees use mud, small pebbles and sand, resin or chewed-up leaves to line and seal their nests. Some mason bees nest only in empty snail shells! Carder bees gather fluff from certain plants and animals, chewing it to make a kind of felt to line their nests. Carpenter bees dig holes in wood and plant stems, using bits of the plant for lining and sealing the nests.

MAPPING THE WORLD

Bees have very small brains. For example, a honey bee's brain is about the size of a sesame seed and contains about one million *neurons*—compared to the 100 billion neurons in a human brain. But they sure are smart! All bees have to leave the nest at some point to find flowers that will provide them with nectar and pollen. Some bees only travel a short distance from the nest, but some, like honey bees, can travel several kilometers (or miles). So how do they find their way back?

First, bees memorize important landmarks (a particular plant or a twig) near the nest. The bee does this by flying in a figure-eight pattern in front of the nest entrance. Gradually, the bee flies in a bigger pattern, going farther from the nest and higher, memorizing larger landmarks. Every afternoon in

When bees go out searching for food, they have to remember how to get back to their nest—as many as several kilometers away.
ANATOLICH/SHUTTERSTOCK.COM

spring and summer, you can see honey bees doing this in front of every healthy hive. *Beekeepers* call it the *orientation flight*.

Next, the bee uses the position of the sun in relation to the nest entrance. Even when the sun is hidden by clouds and its position changes in the sky over the course of the day and the seasons, bees are able to use it as a compass. Don't you wish you could do that?

ANYTHING BUT BUMBLING

When you think of a bee, what kind of bee do you picture? Many people think of bumble bees, the fat, furry, colorful bees that you've probably seen buzzing from flower to flower in spring and summer.

There are only about 250 species of bumble bees around the world, and only forty-six in North America. But native bumble bees are found from deserts and tropical forests to Arctic tundra, in urban areas and at the tops of high mountains.

If a bumble bee doesn't eat pollen or nectar for more than 40 minutes, she will run out of energy to fly. ATAREL/DREAMSTIME.COM

All Abuzz

After I got my first hive of honey bees, I began to be much more aware of bees, not just in my garden but everywhere. I was amazed at how many different kinds there are! I especially love the little bumble bees with the orange bums. Now I keep a small pile of brush in a back corner of the garden, and leave some soil bare rather than covering it in mulch, to provide nesting sites for native bees. I also have two bumble bee boxes, although no bees have used them yet.

Every spring I watch to see if anyone has taken up residence in this luxury bumble bee house. CHRISTOPHER BUTTERFIELD

The oldest known fossilized bee was found in the 1980s in a piece of amber (hardened tree resin) from New Jersey. It is a stingless bee, very similar to a modern stingless bee, but it is more than 83 million years old! This means that there were bees in the last 23 million years of the dinosaurs.

Akai scrapes the wax cappings before we extract the honey. CHRISTOPHER BUTTERFIELD

Bumble bees are social bees. Queens, female workers and males have different jobs in the colony, cooperating with each other to *forage* for food, look after the young and protect the nest.

Bumble bee colonies die at the end of the summer, with the exception of mated females, called *queens*, who hibernate for the winter. In spring, they emerge from *hibernation* and begin to search for a nest. Bumble bees do not make their own nests, but look for abandoned mouse dens, hollow logs, tall grass and even holes in people's houses and other buildings.

When the queen has found a nest, she uses her jaws and legs to shape wax produced by glands in her abdomen into a honeypot for storing nectar. Then she lays her eggs on a ball of pollen moistened with nectar. When the eggs hatch, the larvae feed on the pollen, and the queen has to work hard to take care of them, somehow keeping them warm and finding more food at the same time. After two weeks, the larvae spin silk cocoons and become pupae. Another two weeks later, adult bees emerge and begin to forage for food. Then the queen can stay in the nest and take care of the next bunch of youngsters.

Later in the summer, the queen starts laying special eggs that will become either new queens or males that will mate with them. At the end of the summer, all but the newly mated females die, and the cycle begins again.

SWEET BEES

The honey that we humans love to eat is made by honey bees. There are only eleven honey bee species in the world. None are native to North or South America. The species that is used most for producing honey came from Europe and North Africa, and has been taken to many other parts of the world by humans with a sweet tooth.

Sugar as we know it, made from sugar cane, didn't reach Europe until about 700 years ago. Until then, honey was the only sweetener available. People often kept a hive in their garden so that they would have their own supply of honey. When the Europeans began to settle in North America, they brought honey bee hives with them on ships. Most people believe that honey was introduced to North America by settlers in about 1638. But others think that Irish or Viking travelers brought bees with them as early as AD 800 or 900.

Did you know that other bees make honey too? About 300 species of bees called stingless bees make and store honey in wax, not unlike honey bees. They are found in the tropics, especially in Central and South America. The indigenous peoples of Central America keep Mayan stingless bees in traditional hives made from hollow logs or clay. When Christopher Columbus landed in Cuba, he was presented with gifts of honey—from stingless bees.

We'll find out more about honey bees in Chapter 3.

A Mexican woman opens the end of a hollow log to get honey from a hive of stingless bees. ERIC TOURNERET

All Abuzz

When we got our first honey bee hive, John wanted to show me what a sting feels like. I was scared. But when he put a bee on my hand and forced her to sting me, it barely hurt at all. John showed me how to scrape the stinger off my skin, rather than pulling it out and squeezing more venom in. I still wear a veil and gloves to work with my hives though!

A honey bee's stinger has a sac of venom attached. Scrape the stinger off with your fingernail, rather than pulling it out.
LADISLAV VOZELJ/DREAMSTIME.COM

CHAPTER TWO

Bees at Work

THE BIRDS AND THE BEES

Bees have a very important job in both nature and agriculture: pollinating plants. Most plants, including many of the plants that we humans use for food, need to have their pollen moved from plant to plant in order to reproduce.

Flowering plants have both male and female parts. The male part of a flower (the *stamen*), produces *pollen*, a fine powder that contains the plant's genetic information, or DNA. When the pollen is moved from the stamen on one plant to the female part of a flower (the *pistil*) on another plant of the same kind, that plant will make seeds and fruit. This is called *pollination*. Since plants are rooted to the spot, they need some way to move the pollen from plant to plant.

Some plants, like many grasses and *conifers* (trees with needles and cones), count on the wind to move their pollen. But most rely on animals to carry the pollen from flower to flower. Flies, beetles, butterflies, moths, hummingbirds, bats and even lemurs move pollen, but bees do it best.

Most plants need pollinators like bees to carry pollen from one flower to another so that they can create seeds and fruit.
TUNART/ISTOCK.COM

A HAPPY ACCIDENT

Animals that pollinate plants are called *pollinators*. But pollinators don't pollinate plants on purpose. They visit plants for other reasons.

Often they are looking for food, both for themselves and for their offspring. Pollen provides protein and other important nutrients for bees. Plants also produce *nectar*, a sweet liquid that attracts pollinators, who use it for energy.

Some pollinators visit flowers to find a mate, while others visit to gather oils from the flower to make perfume that will help them attract a mate.

Whatever their reason for visiting the flowers, bees get grains of pollen stuck to their body. When they visit the next flower, some of the grains of pollen rub off—pollination accomplished!

BEE FACT: Some flowers need to be vibrated to release their pollen. Bumble bees and several other wild bees do this by holding on to the flower and vibrating their flight muscles without flapping their wings. Since the vibration makes a buzzing sound, this is called *buzz pollination*.

If you see a really big bumble bee in early spring, it is probably a queen searching for food for herself and her young. TROFIMOV DENIS/SHUTTERSTOCK.COM

IT'S GOOD TO BE HAIRY

What makes bees such good pollinators?

Apart from a few wasp species, it is only bees that deliberately gather pollen to take back to their nests and feed to their young. As well, bees will visit only one kind of plant on a foraging trip. A female bee may visit hundreds of flowers of the same type on a single trip, transferring pollen along the way. If you watch bees in a garden, you will never see them going from, say, a dandelion to a daisy.

And then there is the hair. As bees evolved from their smoother ancestors, the wasps, they developed special branched hairs just for holding pollen. Pollen grains are sticky or oily, and some even have little spikes on them, to help them stick to the feathery hairs on the bee.

Believe it or not, the pollen grains also have a slight electric charge (negative), and bees develop the opposite charge (positive) while they are flying. The positive and negative charges attract, like magnets, and help the pollen stick to the bees as they fly.

The next time you see a bee on a flower, look closely. You will probably see yellow dust on it: that is the pollen, and you'll know that the bee is doing her important work.

THANK YOU, BEES

Many of the foods we eat come from plants that are pollinated by bees, including fruits, vegetables, nuts and seeds. Without bees, for example, we would have no apples, squash, almonds or sunflower seeds. In Canada and the United States, farmers grow more than 100 crop plants that rely on pollinators. Around the world, that number grows to more than 400. In fact, about every third bite of the food we eat and drink every day is from plants

BEE FACT: A worker honey bee's wings beat more than 400 times per second. This is what makes bees buzz, but it also allows them to fly fast—up to 30 kilometers per hour (19 miles per hour)—even when they are fully loaded with nectar or pollen.

Tom uses bumble bees to pollinate the tomatoes, eggplants and other plants in the Sun Wing greenhouses near Victoria.
MERRIE-ELLEN WILCOX

18

Hundreds of beehives are being unloaded from flatbed trucks, so the bees can pollinate this almond orchard in California. ERIC TOURNERET

that need a pollinator. Can you imagine what would happen if the bees didn't do their work?

It wasn't until the twentieth century that people began to understand the role of pollinators in agriculture and find ways to put them to work. Until quite recently, the only pollinators that could be "managed" by people and kept in moveable hives were honey bees and some of the stingless bees. As many small family farms became bigger farms, and big farms began to give way to even larger "industrial" agriculture operations, farmers began to pay beekeepers to bring their honey bee hives to the farm so the bees could pollinate their crops.

Today, millions of honey bee hives are loaded onto large trucks and moved from crop to crop, sometimes thousands of kilometers (miles) across North America. They pollinate the blossoms on apple trees, almond trees, blueberry bushes and many other important crops worth billions of dollars per year.

NOT JUST HONEY (BEES)

But honey bees are having problems. The unhealthy lifestyle that *industrial agriculture* creates for them, along with *pesticides* (poisons used to kill insects and weeds) and some nasty pests and diseases, are killing honey bees at a worrying rate. (In Chapter 4, we'll talk more about the problems that all bees are facing.)

Fortunately, honey bees aren't the only bees that can be used for pollinating food crops. In fact, other bees can often do the job better than honey bees can. Of the 100 or so crops pollinated by bees in North America, only about fifteen are pollinated only by honey bees. The rest are pollinated by wild bees and other animals. Farmers around the world are finding new ways to use bees other than honey bees to pollinate their crops.

The first time this was done was in 1885. There were no native bees in New Zealand that would pollinate clover, a plant

All Abuzz

One of the things I love about looking inside a hive is seeing all the colors of pollen that the bees have brought home. A lot of pollen is yellow or orange, but some plants have other colors. My friend Shirley, who helps me with my bees, studied the pollen to find out which colors come from which plants. So now when I see dark red pollen in spring, I know it's from the flowers on the chestnut trees down the hill. Emerald green is from tulips. And the almost-black pollen that the bees bring later in the summer is from fireweed.

Doesn't this pollen look like candy?
VLADIMIRKIM3722/DEPOSITPHOTOS.COM

that is used to feed cattle and sheep. So four bumble bee species were introduced from England. The experiment was a success: today New Zealand has a lot of cows and sheep, all happily eating clover, thanks to the bumble bees!

Sometimes native bees can be used where they are, without creating artificial homes to move them around in. For example, because squash and pumpkins are native to the Americas, there are native bees that pollinate them. You guessed it: they're called squash bees! Most of the squash and pumpkins that people grow in their own gardens are pollinated by these native bees. And even farmers who grow large amounts of these crops may not need any help from honey bees.

Other kinds of bees will nest in artificial homes that people set up where the bees are needed. For example, an important native bee that is being used in agriculture in different parts of the world is the mason bee. Lots of gardeners where I live are using the blue orchard mason bee for pollination. They provide homes for the bees made from paper tubes or drilled wood or plastic, and store them safely over the winter in a wooden box in a cool, dry place.

North American farmers are using the blue orchard mason bee to pollinate almonds, apples, cherries, pears and plums. In Japan, farmers have been using the native horn-faced mason bee for apple pollination for more than fifty years, and it is now being used in China, Korea and the United States.

Scientists are working hard to learn more about other bees that can be used for pollination, as the honey bee and even many wild bees struggle to survive.

EVEN FISH DEPEND ON BEES

Humans aren't the only creatures who depend on bees for the food we eat. All flowering plants, not just food crops, need to be pollinated. That means that plants in nature rely on bees in

New Zealand has 3 million people and 60 million sheep—all because of some bumble bees brought from England to pollinate clover. PAHHAM/ISTOCK.COM

Can you believe that this giant pumpkin grew from one small flower that was pollinated by one very small squash bee? LINDA KLOOSTERHOF/ISTOCK.COM

Doesn't this look like a happy place for honey bees? Traditional hives (left and middle) on an old family farm in Slovenia. ERIC TOURNERET

order to continue to exist—as do the birds and mammals that rely on those plants for food.

About a quarter of all birds eat the fruits and seeds of plants that are pollinated by bees and other animals. In late summer, even a grizzly bear's diet may consist of almost two-thirds fruit!

All of the living things that depend on each other in some way—from tiny bacteria in soil and water to huge grizzly bears—form an intricate web called an *ecosystem*. Sometimes an entire ecosystem can depend on bees. For example, some plants help to prevent stream and river banks from eroding, keeping the water clean for fish and other things that live there. And those plants depend on pollinators.

If a type of plant can't grow anymore, perhaps because something in the environment has changed, scientists need to understand and take care of the plant's pollinators as well in order to find ways to save the plant.

Even this grizzly bear depends on bees, which pollinate the fruits and berries that make up much of its late-summer diet.
DABURKE/DREAMSTIME.COM

All Abuzz

One fall day after my first year of beekeeping, a man came to our door. He was carrying a paper bag full of beautiful apples, which he handed to me. He explained that he lived nearby and had heard that I was keeping honey bees. His neighbor's apple tree had produced a large crop of apples for the first time. They were sure it was because the honey bees had pollinated the apple blossoms in the spring, so they wanted to thank me. I'm sure they were the best apples I've ever tasted!

Bees pollinating apple blossoms in the spring means lovely apples in the fall.
MOBI68/DREAMSTIME.COM

23

CHAPTER THREE

Life in the Hive

OLD FRIENDS

Of all the bees on the planet, honey bees have always been the most loved by humans. The first known record of people harvesting honey from wild bees is a 6,000-year-old cave painting in Spain. Both the ancient Egyptians and the Chinese kept bees in hives 4,000 years ago. The ancient Greeks believed honey to be the food of the gods. The first alcoholic drink, made from fermented honey and known as *mead*, was used in Africa, China and Europe thousands of years ago. Bees and honey also had important roles in the Mayan and Aztec civilizations.

Our love for bees even shapes our languages. For example, in the Slovenian language there are two words for death: one is used only for humans and bees, and the other is used for all other creatures. And in English we have lots of expressions that refer to bees, such as "He is busy as a bee," "She's got a bee in her bonnet" and "I think you're the bee's knees." Can you think of any others?

Honey bees have always fascinated human beings, appearing in some of the oldest cave paintings—and in storybook pictures like this one. ARCHIVE.ORG

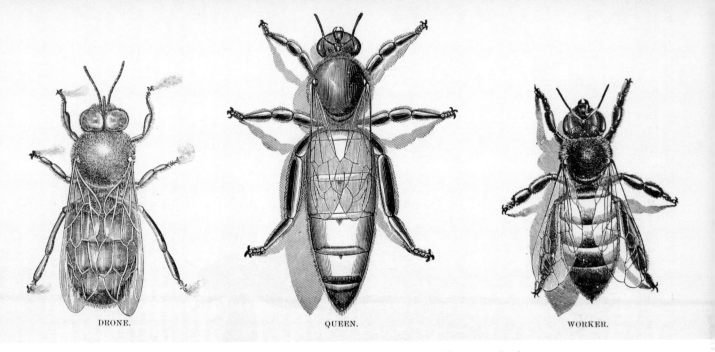

DRONE. QUEEN. WORKER.

The queen honey bee is much bigger than the male drone and female worker bee. The drone is fatter than the worker and doesn't have a stinger. VINTAGEGRAPHICS.OHSONIFTY.COM

THAT'S A LOT OF BEES!

Honey bees can live in the wild in places like hollow trees, but most now live in hives that are looked after by beekeepers. Honey bees are social bees, and each colony, whether in the wild or in a hive, has one queen, a few male bees (called *drones*) and many female worker bees.

In early spring, the queen begins to lay eggs—up to 2,000 a day—and will continue to lay eggs until fall. The population of the hive grows quickly, and by early summer the hive might contain as many as 60,000 bees!

In the winter, the workers form a cluster around the queen to keep her warm. The bees on the outside of the cluster vibrate their wings to generate heat, and when they are tired or cold, they are replaced by bees from inside the cluster. If the bees are healthy and have enough to eat, the queen and a small population will survive until the spring, when the queen will start to lay eggs again.

The queen bee's only job is to lay eggs, one in each cell. Young nurse bees are always nearby, taking care of her. LEHRER/SHUTTERSTOCK.COM

WORK, WORK, WORK

In a honey bee hive, everyone has specific jobs to do.

The queen has only one job, but it's a big one. She lays eggs, one in each hexagonal cell of the wax honeycomb. A queen bee can live for as long as five years, and over the course of her life she can lay as many as a million eggs.

Like the queen, the drones have just one job. They exist only to mate with a new queen. The rest of the time they just laze about, eating honey, while everyone else in the hive works. Sounds like fun, right? But at the end of the summer, since the honey supply has to last for the whole winter, the other bees toss the drones that are still alive right out of the hive, and that's it for them.

The worker bees do everything else in the hive. The most amazing thing is that their age determines the jobs they do. For the first two days of her life, the worker bee cleans the cell she emerged from and helps keep the eggs, larvae and pupae warm.

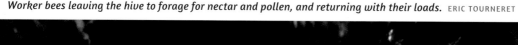

Worker bees leaving the hive to forage for nectar and pollen, and returning with their loads. ERIC TOURNERET

For the next 7 days, she is a nurse bee, feeding the larvae. When she is about 12 days old, the worker bee is able to produce wax from special glands in her abdomen, so she builds or repairs comb, as well as moving food around inside the hive. At about 18 days, she becomes a guard bee at the entrance to the hive. At 22 days, she finally becomes a forager and begins to leave the hive to collect pollen, nectar and water. She dies when she is between 35 and 45 days old, worn out from all that work. That's a lot to accomplish in a short time!

The white stuff in this queen cell is royal jelly, which turns a regular honey bee egg into a queen in just 16 days. ERIC TOURNERET

ROYAL JELLY

In the spring, when the population in a hive is quickly growing and it starts to get crowded, the bees begin to make new queens. First, they make a special, bigger wax cell that hangs down from the honeycomb and looks like a peanut shell. Then they take a regular egg laid by the queen and put it in the cell with some

All Abuzz

One spring afternoon, Akai knocked at my door and told me that my bees had swarmed—right into my neighbor's car! They had flown through a tiny hole into a big ventilation tube under the hood. I asked another beekeeper for help, and the next day he came with a special vacuum cleaner to try to suck the bees out. It took a few tries and another two days to get the queen out of the tube and into a new hive, which we put beside the car, so that all the remaining bees would follow her out of the tube.

Some of the bees came out each day when the sun made it too hot in the tube. Fortunately, my neighbor didn't need his car!
MERRIE-ELLEN WILCOX

The bees in this swarm have left the hive and are pausing on their way to a new home.
WIKIPEDIA.COM

BEE FACT: There is a tradition in Europe and the United Kingdom called "telling the bees." When a beekeeper dies, the bees must be told, as it was believed that otherwise they too would decline and die. In the past, bees were also told about births and weddings, and about public news, like the coronation of a new king.

royal jelly (also known as *bee milk*), a mixture of sugar, pollen and nutrients produced by glands in their head. They keep feeding royal jelly to the queen-to-be until she emerges from her cell sixteen days later.

A few days after a new queen emerges from her cell, she must do her mating flight. And this is where those lazy drones come in. As the young queen flies, drones in the area chase her and mate with her—in the air! She may do more than one flight and will mate with several drones, who die right after mating. Once a queen has mated, she can lay eggs for the rest of her life.

SWARM ALERT!

While the new queen is maturing in her wax cell, the old queen flies away to a new home. Scout bees will have been searching for an ideal spot, usually in a cavity like a hollow tree or a chimney. The scouts spend a lot of time examining each possible site, flying both inside and outside it, and crawling on every surface. Once they have found a good home, the queen and about half of the bees leave the hive all at once. They land nearby, gradually forming a big cluster. This is called a *swarm*. Swarming is how honey bees make new colonies in order to increase their population.

Have you ever seen a swarm? It only takes a few minutes, but it's quite dramatic, with about 25,000 bees flying noisily in the air together! People often think a swarm is dangerous, but it's not. The bees fill up on honey in the hive before they take flight, so they are full and content, and just want to stick with their queen.

After a day or two in their cluster, the queen and her bees will fly again, this time to the new home that the scouts have found. Ideally, though, a beekeeper will come and catch all the bees first and set them up in a new hive.

To make a "bee beard," the beekeeper puts a queen and some young bees on a calm volunteer. DEB ALPERIN/GETTYIMAGES.COM

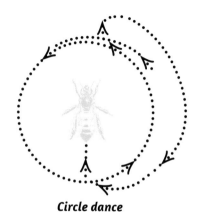

Circle dance

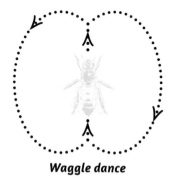

Waggle dance

DANCING BEES

How do honey bees tell each other about things like a new home? How do they find the flowers they need to visit for gathering nectar and pollen? They talk to each other—not with words but by dancing!

When a foraging honey bee has found a good source of nectar or pollen, she flies back to the hive and performs a dance on one of the combs near the entrance. The pattern of the dance tells the other bees the exact direction and distance of the flowers. The two best-known dances are the circle dance and the waggle dance.

If the bee has found a source of food close to the hive, she walks quickly in small circles, reversing her direction after each circle or two and stopping every few seconds to pass nectar to the other bees that are gathered around. This is the circle dance.

All Abuzz

There are few things as magical as looking in a honey bee hive on a warm summer day. There are many organizations around the world that are sharing that magic with others to help make their lives better. Some are working with people in places like Africa, using beekeeping to improve pollination on their farms and increase their income with honey and wax. Others, like Hives for Humanity, are training people who live in poor neighborhoods in cities like Vancouver to keep honey bees, giving them skills and an income.

People making beekeeping equipment for Hives for Humanity, in Vancouver.
HIVES FOR HUMANITY

If the bee has found food farther away from the hive, she does the more complicated waggle dance. She moves in a figure eight, moving her body from side to side and "waggling" her abdomen, telling the bees about the exact direction, distance and quality of the food.

The bees use other dances as well, vibrating their bodies and walking in a specific pattern to communicate about things like swarming.

Many beekeepers use a smoker like this boy has because smoke calms the bees in the hive.
NKAROL/DREAMSTIME.COM

WHAT BEEKEEPERS DO

You might be wondering why bees need "keepers" at all, since they are already so good at what they do.

Traditionally, people kept bees so they could have their own source of honey and wax. Some people then started having lots of hives so that they could sell honey and wax to others. In the twentieth century, some of these "commercial" beekeepers started to sell the pollination services of their bees, transporting their hives from farm to farm and crop to crop for a fee.

Linnea has taken one of about 30 frames out of a hive to check on the bees.
NADINE FIEDLER/CATLIN GABEL SCHOOL

These young Maori women are processing manuka honey in New Zealand.

But many beekeepers, like me, just keep bees as a hobby, because the bees are so fascinating. We never stop learning about our little golden friends!

Whether we are commercial or hobbyist beekeepers, many of our tasks are the same. In the early spring, we open the hives to see if the bees have survived the winter. Sometimes they have run out of honey, so we need to feed them honey or sugar. Later in the spring, we try to make sure that they aren't going to swarm; if they do, we try to retrieve the swarm and start a new hive. In the summer, we take the honey out of the hive. Depending on the type of hive we are using, this involves taking the honeycomb out of the hive and then extracting and filtering the honey. In the fall, we try to make sure that the bees have enough honey for the winter and that the hive is well insulated from the cold and damp. In the winter, we clean our tools and build new equipment if we need it, always wondering if our "girls" are okay.

Depending on where their hives are, many beekeepers have to protect them from other animals who like honey, such as mice, skunks and bears. A new task that beekeepers everywhere must do all the time is treating the bees for parasites and diseases. (More about that in Chapter 4.)

GOOD MEDICINE

People have loved honey bees for thousands of years, mainly because of what the bees produce. Honey has been used not just for its sweetness, but also as medicine. For example, people have long used honey to soothe sore throats and coughs, and sometimes to treat wounds.

Scientists now understand that honey can be good medicine because of two special qualities. First, honey contains traces of hydrogen peroxide, which is an *antiseptic*. (You might have used hydrogen peroxide to clean cuts and scrapes.) But like other strong mixtures of sugar, honey also attracts and absorbs moisture. It kills bacteria by absorbing all the moisture that bacteria need to survive. A honey from New Zealand, called *manuka honey*, is now used in bandages and dressings for wounds and burns because it is especially good at killing bacteria.

There are other important products of the hive that people believe have medicinal properties. Some people use pollen collected by honey bees to treat health problems like allergies. Others use *propolis*—dark red sticky stuff that bees make from tree resin to seal up cracks and holes in the hive—to fight colds and sore throats. Recent research has shown that royal jelly may help prevent deposits of fat clogging up human arteries. Even bee venom—the stuff that makes a bee sting sting—is used by people to treat or prevent arthritis.

Of course, beeswax has been used for thousands of years to make candles. It is also used to make healing salves and even cosmetics, as well as for casting metal objects like jewelry. Today it is used to cast large metal objects, including the blades inside jet engines!

Got a sore throat or a cough? Try taking a spoonful of manuka honey—or any good, unpasteurized local honey.
LAZINGBEE/ISTOCK.COM

BEE FACT: Honey is a great preservative. It never goes bad. Honey has been found in Egyptian tombs that are more than 3,000 years old, and it can still be eaten!

CHAPTER FOUR

Keeping the Bees in Flight

Pesticides can be very harmful to bees—as well as other insects, birds, and animals.
MODFOS/DREAMSTIME.COM

BEES ARE GETTING STUNG

As I've mentioned in other chapters, and as you might have heard in the news, honey bees are in trouble. They have been dying in huge numbers around the world. Many commercial beekeepers have had to close their businesses because of their losses. And some hobbyists have given up in frustration.

Scientists still aren't sure whether there is a single cause of these problems or many causes. But we do know that there are several different things that are harmful to honey bees.

Bees that have to travel long distances on flatbed trucks to pollinate different crops are already stressed. Imagine what it's like for bees that are usually free to roam outside, being sealed inside their hives, fed on corn syrup or sugar water, and bounced around on the back of a flatbed truck for days on end. Once they arrive, they have a diet of only one thing for weeks at a time (apple blossoms, almond blossoms, blueberry blossoms), rather than all the different foods that they would have in a more natural environment.

People all over the world, like these protesters in Tampa, Florida, are doing what they can to stop the use of harmful pesticides. KRIZ PARTRIDGE/BEE AGAINST MONSANTO

Wherever they are, honey bees can be exposed to a variety of poisons as they move from plant to plant. For example, they can come into contact with *insecticides*, which are used to kill insect pests, and *herbicides*, which are used to kill weeds. These chemicals can either kill bees right away or build up gradually in the honey and wax in a hive, making the bees sick and weak. One class of insecticides, called *neonicotinoids* (neo-**ni**-co-teen-**oyds**), is thought to be especially harmful to honey bees. They are similar to the nicotine in cigarettes; are used to kill insects that suck and chew plants, insects in soil, and fleas on animals; and are sprayed on soil and on the seeds and plants of many crops. Some "neonics" have been banned in Europe, but not in North America.

The brown spot on this honey bee is a varroa mite. Mites can cause a whole colony to die in just a few months. SCIENCEPHOTO.COM

As if that weren't enough, honey bees around the world are dealing with a variety of parasites and diseases. One of the most common is the *varroa mite*, whose formal name is *Varroa destructor*. It's a small crablike insect that you can actually see on

In cities, as well as in places where there is logging or industrial agriculture, wild bees have few places to nest and little food to eat. GQP/ISTOCK.COM

the bees if you look closely. The varroa mite itself only weakens the bees, but it also carries several diseases that can kill them, such as deformed wing virus.

WILD BEES TOO

It's not just honey bees that are in trouble. Many wild bees are threatened too. Not surprisingly, some of the same kinds of things that harm honey bees also harm wild bees—especially pesticides. But there is another problem for wild bees that isn't a problem for honey bees, and that is the loss of *habitat*, places where bees can nest and find the foods they need.

Since most honey bees live in hives, and the hives are usually in places where there is lots of pollen and nectar available for them to eat, they don't need to worry too much about finding places to live and enough food for themselves and their offspring. Not true for wild bees.

In urban and suburban areas, where much of the ground is covered in pavement, concrete, lawns or buildings, bees that live in or on the ground have nowhere to make their nests and none of the native plants they need for pollen and nectar. Large-scale industrial farming also destroys bee habitat, as does logging in forests.

HELPING THE HELPERS

The bees who do so much for us and for the world we live in need our help. It's really important to understand and take care of them, not just because we rely on them for much of our food, but because many of the plants and creatures in our environment do as well.

Around the world, people are becoming more aware of bees and our dependence on them, and are working to save bees in all kinds of different ways. Scientists are doing research to

BEE FACT: Even in areas that are not affected by *urbanization*, industrial agriculture or logging, plants from other places, called *invasive species*, can crowd out the native plants that bees need for food and nesting.

In some parts of China, there are so few bees left that people have to pollinate fruit trees by hand. ERIC TOURNERET

All Abuzz

One fall, both of my hives died. They were sick because of varroa mites, and the yellow jackets (wasps) finished them off. I was so sad and frustrated that I decided to pack it in as a beekeeper. No more bees for me. But when the spring came, and the hives sat there empty, with no bees coming and going in the sunshine, I missed them too much. I got more bees, and now it's hard to imagine life without them. So be careful: beekeeping can be addictive!

A fellow beekeeper brought me a swarm of bees that he had caught, and we put them into my hive. CHRISTOPHER BUTTERFIELD

37

Toronto's Royal York Hotel was the first hotel in the world to have beehives on its roof. THE FAIRMONT ROYAL YORK

better understand bees, especially wild bees, so that we will know what they need to survive. Honey bees have long been a focus of research, but scientists are working hard to understand exactly why they are dying in such large numbers.

Even in the world's largest cities, many people are keeping honey bees, both at home and in public places. In Paris, for example, there are hives on the rooftops of the opera house, Notre Dame Cathedral and the National Assembly. Many major hotels in North America, as well as in China and Kenya, have hives on their rooftops or in their gardens. The Royal York Hotel in Toronto even has a rooftop "bee hotel" for native bees.

In cities and in rural areas alike, people are planting pollinator gardens and meadows containing plants that bees need. They leave areas where wild bees can nest and *overwinter*. People are also pledging not to use harmful pesticides and are petitioning their governments to restrict or ban them.

Farmers are helping, too, by not using chemicals at all or using them only if absolutely necessary, having native wild-flowers growing at the edges of their fields, and even leaving a part of each field unplanted (or *fallow*) every year.

BEE-FRIENDLY KIDS

Kids are helping bees in lots of ways, and you can too! Here are some things that you can do to help make wherever you live more bee-friendly.

Keep your eyes and ears open

In the spring and summer, wherever you go, watch and listen for bees. Even in the middle of the biggest cities, if there are plants, flowers or trees, there will likely be bees, since plants need bees and bees need plants. Once you begin to be aware of bees,

Pollinator gardens are a great way to support wild bees. PHILIPDYER/ISTOCK.COM

39

If you can't find any native plants, here are some plants that many bees love and that are available at most garden centers:

- basil
- borage
- catnip
- common sunflower
- cosmos
- lavender
- mint
- oregano
- rosemary
- Russian sage
- stonecrop

you'll see them everywhere. You'll be amazed at how many different kinds of bees you can spot! And remember, as long as you are quiet and still, bees won't be worried about you, so they won't sting.

Look for pollen on a bee. It might have a yellow dusting all over its body. If it's a honey bee or a bumble bee, it might also be carrying a yellow or orange ball on each of its back legs.

Keep your eyes on the ground too. Wherever there is bare soil—even in a schoolyard or a playground—watch for low-flying bees. Wild bees might be searching for their nests. Or if you find a small hole in the ground, watch it quietly for a few minutes. You might see a bee returning to the nest, loaded with nectar and pollen.

Plant a garden

Even if you live in a big city, you can make your area friendlier for bees. Ask your parents if you can plant some flowers. If you are lucky enough to have a backyard, maybe you can even have a corner of it to make your own pollinator garden. If you don't have a backyard, try planting flowers in pots, maybe on a balcony or in a courtyard.

Try to use *native* plants, the plants that have always grown naturally where you live, because they are much more likely to be useful to the native bees. Since native plants have adapted to the climate and other conditions, they should grow quite quickly once they get started. (Go online or to the library to find out about the native plants in your area.)

Don't spray

If your family's home has a lawn or a garden, ask your parents not to use chemical pesticides unless they absolutely have to, or to use as little as possible.

Maybe they will even let you let the dandelions grow in your lawn! Dandelion flowers are great for bees, and if you just pull the flowers off before they go to seed and turn into fluff-puffs, they won't spread like crazy.

Give them a home

Providing places for wild bees to nest can be as easy as just leaving some bare soil. If your parents use mulch (ground-up wood and bark) on a garden in order to keep the weeds down and the moisture in, ask them if they will leave an area mulch-free. You might have to volunteer to do the weeding, but then you'll get to watch for bees nesting in the ground!

For bees that nest in tubes, a nesting site could be something as simple as a small bundle of bamboo sticks tied together. You can also use paper tubes or (with help!) drill holes in logs or other dead wood. You can even build a bumble bee house out of an upside-down flower pot and a few other easy-to-find materials. It may take a while for the home to be occupied, so be patient!

A small pile of sticks and branches in an unused corner somewhere can also be a great place for bees to overwinter, since they often don't use their nests for hibernation.

You can find more information about how to make bee housing in many of the resources at the back of this book.

Bring it to school

Lots of schools and community groups are growing pollinator meadows. A pollinator meadow doesn't have to be big to attract and provide food for bees. And it doesn't have to cost a lot. You can start small and add on. If you think this would be a good idea for your class or your school, talk to your teachers. Again, you can find lots of information about how to create a meadow in the books and websites listed at the back of the book.

Some schools even have their own honey bee hives and sell their honey and wax to people in their community.

If you and your class are interested in learning more about bees, ask your teacher to invite an entomologist to come and

Some people are helping wild bees by building homes for them—in all shapes and sizes—in their backyards.
HSVRS/ISTOCK.COM

talk to your class. If it's honey bees you're interested in, you could invite a beekeeper to your school, or arrange a field trip to see some honey bee hives.

Support our farmers

Another way to be bee-friendly is to support local farmers. Even if you live in a big city, ask your parents to take you to a farmers' market so you can see and taste all the wonderful things that local farmers grow. If you live in a smaller town or a rural area, there might be farms nearby that have farm stands where they sell their produce. Many farmers, especially those with small and organic farms, are using bee-friendly methods. If you ask, a farmer will probably be happy to tell or even show you what he or she is doing for the bees.

Farmers can get their farms certified as bee-friendly by the Pollinator Partnership.
LAURIE DAVIES ADAMS/POLLINATOR PARTNERSHIP

Local farmers with smaller farms are more likely than large industrial farms to use bee-friendly practices. JIM WEST/ALAMY

Buy local, honey!

If you are really curious about honey bees, or think you might even want to be a beekeeper, talk to someone who is selling honey at a local farmers' market. If you can, buy a little of the honey.

If the person selling the honey is the beekeeper, ask if you can maybe take a look at his or her hives sometime. Beekeepers often have extra veils and gloves so that you can get close to a hive safely. There's no age limit to becoming a beekeeper, as long as you have someone to help you get started.

If you don't have a market in your area, most places have a local beekeepers' association that you can contact. You might be able to attend a meeting, or just call someone in the group who can give you the name of a beekeeper to talk to. Like entomologists and farmers (and anyone else who loves what they do), beekeepers love to share what they know!

Annie is selling my honey at our neighborhood farmers' market. MERRIE-ELLEN WILCOX

BEE FACT: Chemicals aren't used only in agriculture. In fact, in many places more pesticides are used in urban areas than on farms.

All Abuzz

One honey bee makes only one-twelfth of a teaspoon of honey in her life. To produce one pound (about half a kilogram) of honey, honey bees have to visit more than two million flowers and travel more than 88,500 kilometers (55,000 miles). Before I heard that, I had no idea how valuable honey is. When I eat honey now—usually on bread or yogurt, or just with a spoon—I always think about how hard the bees worked to make it and thank them for sharing their food with me.

Nate fills a jar with honey. Sweet, sticky work! MERRIE-ELLEN WILCOX

Resources

Books

Buchmann, Stephen. *Honey Bees: Letters from the Hive.* New York, NY: Random House, 2010.

Xerces Society. *Attracting Native Pollinators: Protecting North America's Bees and Butterflies.* North Adams, MA: Storey Publishing, 2011.

Websites

The BeeWorld Project: www.ibrabeeworldproject.com

Bumblebee Conservation Trust, Bumble Kids: http://bumblebeeconservation.org/get-involved/bumble-kids

Gardening with Kids: www.kidsgardening.org/node/11941

The Great Sunflower Project: www.greatsunflower.org

Hives for Humanity: http://hivesforhumanity.com

International Pollination Systems: www.pollination.com/bees-in-the-classroom/students

Kids and Bees: www.beegirl.org/#!kidsandbees/sitepage_2

Pollinator Live: http://pollinatorlive.pwnet.org/index.php

Pollinator Partnership: www.pollinator.org

Pollinator Partnership Canada: http://pollinator.org/canada.htm

The Xerces Society for Invertebrate Conservation: www.xerces.org/pollinator-conservation

Acknowledgments

First, huge thanks to Orca for including a book about bees in the wonderful Footprints series—and especially to my editor and friend Sarah Harvey for guiding me through the process, and to Jenn Playford for her beautiful design. Photos of kids with bees aren't easy to find, so thanks to all of you who courageously donned gloves and veil and opened the hives with me, or worked with all that sticky honey, so that we could photograph you: my neighbors, Akai, Nate and Annie; and my nieces Robin and Marijn and their friends Eliza, Sarah and Isabel. I am also grateful to the people and organizations who generously shared their photos: Rob Cruickshank, Brian Scullion, Chris Wieczorek, Catlin Gabel School, Hives for Humanity and the Canadian Hunger Foundation. Special thanks to Éric Tourneret (www.thehoneygatherers.com) for his exquisite photos, and to Michelle Mulder and Mary Rose MacLachlan for their coaching.

None of this would have happened if I hadn't stumbled into beekeeping in the first place. Thank you to my neighbors for welcoming the honey bees and putting up with occasional swarms; Louise Oborne and Doug Rhodes for the Pink Queen adventures; and Shirley Richardson for sharing her love of bees and beekeeping with me. And to my husband, Christopher Butterfield, thank you for telling John Defayette that we had *always* wanted a hive in our garden—and for building equipment, putting out fires, taking photos and loving the bees as much as I do.

Finally, to the honey bees and all their wild cousins, on whom we humans depend for so much: may we understand and treat you better so that you can keep on buzzing.

Glossary

abdomen—the rear part of an insect's body

Africanized bee ("killer" bee)—an aggressive species that resulted from scientists mating European and African honey bees

amber—hardened tree resin, usually a yellow or brown color

antenna (pl. antennae)—on the head of insects and some other animals, one of a pair of slender, movable "feelers" that are sensitive to touch and sometimes to taste and smell

antiseptic—any substance (like hydrogen peroxide) that prevents or stops the growth of bacteria

beekeeper—a person who raises honey bees, as either a hobby or a business

buzz pollination—a type of pollination that bumble bees and some other bees do by holding the flower and vibrating their flight muscles without flapping their wings

carnivore—any creature that eats meat

cocoon—a silky covering that bees (and some other insects and animals) make around themselves for protection while they grow from larva to adult

colony—a group of social bees

compound eye—a type of eye that insects and other invertebrates have, made up of many separate lenses

conifer—a tree that produces cones and that usually has needle-like leaves that stay green all year

corbicula (pollen basket)—a special structure on the hind legs of some female bees, used for carrying pollen

drone—a male honey bee, whose only job is to mate with a queen

ecosystem—a community of living things that interact with each other and the nonliving things in their environment

entomologist—a person who studies insects

fallow—when a field is left unplanted so the soil can rest and regenerate nutrients

forage—to search for food

generalist bees—bees that can easily collect pollen and nectar from a variety of plants

habitat—places where bees can nest and find the foods they need

herbicide—a poison that is used to kill weeds

hibernation—spending the winter sleeping or resting

industrial agriculture—a system of farming that uses very large farms to grow a single crop or very large facilities to produce animals for meat

insecticide—a poison that is used to kill insects

invasive species—plants and animals from other places that can crowd out the plants and animals that are native to a place

larva (pl. larvae)—the stage of an insect's development between egg and pupa

manuka honey—a type of honey from New Zealand that is especially good at killing bacteria

mead—an alcoholic drink made from fermented honey

metamorphosis—a major change in the structure of an animal's body

native—(of plants and animals) living or growing naturally in a particular region

nectar—a sweet liquid produced by plants to attract pollinators

neonicotinoid—a class of insecticide that is especially harmful to honey bees

neuron—a cell that carries messages between the brain and other parts of the body

ocellus (pl. ocelli)—(eye spot) a simple eye with a single lens

orientation flight—a type of flight that bees do to memorize the landscape around their hive or nest

overwinter—to stay alive through the winter

pesticide—a poison that is used to kill insects and weeds

pistil—the female part of a flower

pollen—a fine powder produced by a plant, containing its genetic information, or DNA

pollination—the transfer of pollen from one plant to another so that the plant can reproduce

pollinator—an insect or other animal that carries pollen from one plant to another

propolis—a dark-red sticky substance that honey bees make from tree resin to seal up cracks and holes in the hive

pupa—the stage in an insect's development between larva and adult

royal jelly (bee milk)—a mixture of sugar, pollen and nutrients produced by glands in a honey bee's head, which is fed in small amounts to larvae and in large amounts to queen larvae

scopa (Latin for "broom")—a special structure made of long, stiff hairs on the hind legs of some female bees, used for carrying pollen

specialist bees—bees that can get their food only from specific types of flowers

stamen—the male part of a flower, which produces pollen

swarm—a very large number of honey bees that have left a hive with their queen to find a new home

thorax—the middle section of an insect's body

urbanization—the growth of towns and cities on land that was once wilderness or farmland, and the movement of people from rural to urban areas

varroa mite (Varroa destructor)—a small crablike insect that feeds on honey bees and often carries diseases that can kill bees

Index (continued)

Index